EDGE BOOKS

WAR MACHINES

HIGH MOBILITY VEHICLES

The Humvees

by Nick Healy

Consultant:

Craig MacNab

Director, Public Relations

AM General LLC

South Bend, Indiana

Capstone
press

Mankato, Minnesota

Edge Books are published by Capstone Press,
151 Good Counsel Drive, P.O. Box 669, Mankato, Minnesota 56002.
www.capstonepress.com

Library of Congress Cataloging-in-Publication Data
Healy, Nick.
    High mobility vehicles: the Humvees / by Nick Healy.
    p. cm.—(Edge books. War machines)
    Includes bibliographical references and index.
    ISBN 0-7368-3778-7 (hardcover)
    1. Hummer truck—Juvenile literature. 2. Military trucks—United States—
Juvenile literature. I. Title. II. Edge Books, war machines.
UG618.H43 2005
623.7'4722—dc22   2004013901

Summary: Describes the HMMWV (Humvee), including its history, equipment, weapons, tactics, and future use.

Editorial Credits
Angie Kaelberer, editor; Jason Knudson, set designer; Patrick D. Dentinger, book designer; Jo Miller, photo researcher; Scott Thoms, photo editor

Photo Credits
AM General Corporation LLC/Rob Wurtz, cover, 9, 13, 14–15, 16–17, 26
AP Wide World Photos/US Army/Robert Woodward, 6
Corbis/Bettmann, 8
DVIC/Arnold Kalmanson, 11; LCPL Brandon Gwathney, 23; LCPL E. J. Young, 20; LCPL Kevin C. Quihuis Jr., USMC, 25; LCPL Simon Martin, USMC, 21; Marshall W. Woods, CIV, 22; SGT B. E. Vancise, USMC, 12; SGT Curtis G. Hargrave, USA, 5; SSG William Armstrong, USA, 19
Getty Images Inc./Scott Olson, 28; Time Life Pictures/Robert Yarnall Richie, 7

1 2 3 4 5 6 10 09 08 07 06 05

Table of Contents

CHAPTER 1

The Humvee in Action

Four U.S. Army vehicles stop outside a mansion in northern Iraq. Soldiers rush out of the vehicles. They surround the building. One soldier speaks into a bullhorn. He calls for everyone to come out of the house. His demands are ignored.

A gunfight breaks out when the soldiers try to enter the mansion. Bullets pour out from inside the house. Four soldiers are wounded. The soldiers turn back and call for help.

More vehicles speed to the scene. Some carry eight soldiers on benches in back. Others have machine guns mounted on top. Some have missile launchers. Still others are ambulances. All of the vehicles are Humvees. Their name is short for High Mobility Multipurpose Wheeled Vehicle.

Soldiers in Humvees led a dangerous mission in Iraq.

LEARN ABOUT:

A Humvee mission

Need for the Humvee

History

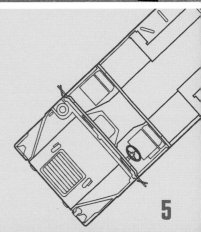

The soldiers are fighting a dangerous enemy.
The two sons of Iraq's former ruler Saddam
Hussein are inside the house. The men are
known to be cruel and violent. The gunfight
rages for more than two hours.

Finally, an order comes to fire antitank
missiles at the mansion. Ten missiles fly from
launchers mounted on Humvees. They strike
the building, and smoke fills the air. All gunfire
from inside stops. The enemy has been defeated.

Tough and Dependable

In 1979, the Army decided to improve its motor vehicles. The Army was still using jeeps and other older trucks. Many of these vehicles had changed little since the 1940s. Army leaders decided they needed a new vehicle.

Before the Humvee, Army vehicles had changed little since the 1940s.

Army leaders wanted many things from the new vehicle. The vehicle had to carry 1.25 tons (1.13 metric tons) of cargo. It had to climb rocky slopes and slosh through flooded valleys. Most of all, the vehicle needed to be sturdy, reliable, and easy to fix.

Building the Humvee

Army leaders asked three companies to build test vehicles. These companies were Teledyne, Chrysler Defense, and AM General.

The Army received its first Humvees in 1985.

Some Humvees are ambulances.

The Army put the three vehicles through about 450 tests. Army members tested the vehicles for strength. They also tested the vehicles' ability to travel through water and over different types of land. Army leaders chose AM General's model.

AM General built 15 styles of Humvees. They included troop carriers, ammunition carriers, ambulances, and armored missile launchers.

Today, the Army has about 100,000 Humvees. The Marine Corps, Navy, and Air Force also use Humvees.

CHAPTER 2

Inside the Humvee

Most Humvees are built around the same type of chassis. This steel frame is covered by an aluminum body.

One Vehicle, Many Uses

The Army uses Humvees in different ways. Many Humvees are designed to carry cargo and soldiers. Others are used as ambulances.

Humvees can be armed with weapons. These weapons include machine guns and grenade launchers. Humvees also carry missiles that destroy tanks and aircraft.

Some Humvee models launch antitank missiles.

LEARN ABOUT:

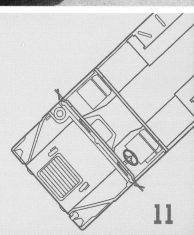

Helicopters use slings made of nylon webbing to carry Humvees.

All-Terrain Vehicle

Humvees are easy to move from place to place. They fit inside some helicopters and airplanes. Other helicopters can carry a Humvee below the aircraft. Slings made of nylon webbing connect the Humvee to the helicopter.

Humvees travel over all types of terrain. The frame is 16 inches (41 centimeters) above the ground. The high frame allows Humvees to rumble over rocks and debris without being damaged.

All Humvees can travel through 2.5 feet (.8 meter) of water. Some Humvees have equipment that lets them drive through 5 feet (1.5 meters) of water. Water may flow into the driver's cab, but the Humvee can keep going.

Humvees have independent four-wheel drive. Each of the four wheels is powered separately. Humvees move as long as one wheel can grip the ground.

Humvees can drive through deep water.

Stable Design

Humvees are stable compared to most other military trucks. Many military trucks have short, narrow wheelbases. They sometimes roll over on sharp turns or steep slopes. Humvees are long and wide. At 6.2 feet (1.9 meters), they are not very tall. This design helps prevent Humvees from rolling over.

Even the Humvee's tires are different from those on other military vehicles. All Humvees have run-flat tires. They can keep going for 30 miles (48 kilometers) on flat tires.

Some Humvees have a Central Tire Inflation System (CTIS). This system allows the driver to change the air pressure in the tires to fit the terrain. The driver uses a control in the cab to add or release air from the tires.

Humvees travel over rough terrain without rolling over.

M1114 Humvee

Function:	Multipurpose wheeled vehicle
Manufacturer:	AM General LLC; armored by O'Gara-Hess and Eisenhardt
Date First Deployed:	1995
Length:	16.4 feet (5 meters)
Height:	6.2 feet (1.9 meters)
Width:	7.5 feet (2.3 meters)
Curb Weight:	9,800 pounds (4,447 kilograms)
Engine:	V-8 turbocharged diesel
Horsepower:	190
Top Speed:	78 miles (125 kilometers) per hour
Range:	275 miles (443 kilometers)

1 **Antenna**

2 **Run-flat tire**

3 **Armored door**

4 **Weapons turret**

5 **Raised air intake**

6 **Weapons mount**

CHAPTER 3

Weapons and Tactics

Humvees are all about power. They have plenty of power under the hood. They deliver firepower on the battlefield. Many Humvees are mounted with guns or missile systems. Others haul large weapons.

Weapons Transport

Some Humvees are called prime movers. They pull howitzers and other large pieces of equipment around the battlefield. Howitzers are large cannons. They sit on a wheeled base that is hooked to a Humvee like a trailer.

Prime movers have a large rack over the driver's cab. The rack holds a camouflage net. The net hides the howitzer from view.

The M1025 Humvee is equipped with a .50-caliber machine gun.

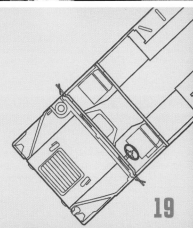

LEARN ABOUT:

Prime movers

TOW missiles

The Avenger

Missile Carrier

The TOW missile is one of the most effective Humvee weapons. Its full name is Tube-launched, Optically-tracked, Wire command-link missile system. TOW launchers are mounted on top of some Humvees.

Two thin wires are attached to a TOW missile. The wires trail behind the fired missile like fishing lines. They carry commands that guide the missile

The TOW missile can hit targets 2 miles (3.2 kilometers) away.

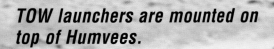

to the target. TOW missiles have a range of about 2 miles (3.2 kilometers).

The TOW missile is known best as an antitank weapon. But it also destroys other types of targets. U.S. soldiers used TOW missiles to end their battle with the sons of former Iraqi leader Saddam Hussein.

Defense Systems

Some Humvees are fitted with an antiaircraft missile system. This type of Humvee is called the Avenger. It has a missile-firing platform turret mounted on its back. The turret fills the place where many Humvees carry soldiers or cargo.

The Avenger's turret holds eight Stinger missiles. Crew members can fire the missiles while the Avenger is moving. They also can fire the missiles by remote control.

Avengers carry Stinger missiles.

Once fired, Stingers sense heat coming from an enemy aircraft's engine. The missiles follow that heat to the aircraft.

A soldier called a gunner operates the turret platform. The platform turret rotates in a full circle. This movement allows the gunner to follow enemy airplanes and helicopters. The Avenger also has a .50-caliber machine gun mounted on the side of the turret.

CHAPTER 4

The Future

AM General keeps changing and improving the Humvee. The Army faces new challenges during times of peace and war. The Humvee will have to meet those changing demands.

Humvees in Iraq

In 2003, Operation Iraqi Freedom showed a need for more heavily armored Humvees. After Saddam Hussein was captured, U.S. soldiers were ordered to keep peace in Iraqi cities. Soon, the soldiers became targets for terrorists.

Standard Humvees provide little protection from terrorist attacks. Bullets go through their thin aluminum bodies. Some standard Humvees have roofs made of stiff cloth called canvas. Others have no roofs at all.

Canvas roofs don't protect crews from enemy bullets.

LEARN ABOUT:

Up-Armored Humvees

Hybrids

Future need

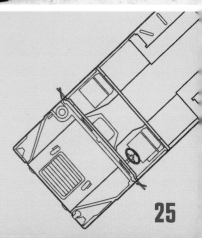

Armor Protection

One type of Humvee provides better protection. Up-Armored Humvees are heavier than standard Humvees because they are covered with tough armor. An Up-Armored Humvee can survive hits from grenades, machine gun bullets,

and land mines. The vehicle may be heavily damaged, but the soldiers inside remain safe.

In early 2004, the Army had about 12,000 Humvees in Iraq. Only about 2,000 of them were Up-Armored Humvees. Army leaders rushed to get more Up-Armored Humvees into Iraq. The leaders also decided to buy 6,000 more of the armored vehicles.

A New Humvee

The Army has tested a diesel-electric hybrid Humvee. These Humvees have both a small diesel engine and an electric motor. They run on a mix of electric and diesel power.

Hybrid vehicles have many benefits. They use less fuel and can travel about 10 miles (16 kilometers) per hour faster than standard Humvees. Hybrid Humvees also have more power for climbing slopes.

Up-Armored Humvees offer protection from many weapons.

A hybrid Humvee could be useful on the battlefield. Electric-powered engines are very quiet. Once parked, a hybrid Humvee becomes an electrical generator. It can provide electric power for other systems. But hybrids will probably not replace standard Humvees any time soon.

After more than 20 years, the Humvee remains the heart of the Army's motor fleet. Army leaders know they can depend on the Humvee during missions around the world.

The H2 is one model of the Hummer.

The Hummer

Only soldiers can drive Humvees, but other people can buy a similar vehicle. The civilian version of the Humvee is called the Hummer.

AM General sold the first H1 Hummers in 1992. Now, AM General makes the vehicles for General Motors, which bought the Hummer brand.

In 2002, General Motors introduced a smaller version of the H1 called the H2. In 2004, a sport-utility truck called the H2 SUT became available.

Hummers are expensive. The H2 and H2 SUT both cost about $50,000. The larger H1 sells for about $100,000.

Glossary

armor (AR-mur)—a protective metal covering

canvas (KAN-vuhss)—a type of strong cloth

cargo (KAR-goh)—the goods carried by a ship, vehicle, or aircraft

chassis (CHASS-ee)—the frame on which the body of a vehicle is built

civilian (si-VIL-yuhn)—a person who is not in the military

fleet (FLEET)—a group of vehicles

hybrid (HYE-brid)—a vehicle that is a combination of two or more other vehicles; Humvee hybrids can run on either diesel fuel or electricity.

mansion (MAN-shuhn)—a large, expensive house

terrain (tuh-RAYN)—ground or land

terrorist (TER-ur-ist)—a person who uses violence and threats to get something from a group of people or a government

turret (TUR-it)—a rotating structure that holds a weapon on top of a military vehicle

Read More

Budd, E. S. *Humvees.* Military Machines at Work. Chanhassen, Minn.: Child's World, 2002.

Green, Michael. *Military Trucks.* Land and Sea. Mankato, Minn.: Capstone Press, 1997.

Morse, Jenifer Corr. *Military Vehicles.* Speed! Woodbridge, Conn.: Blackbirch Press, 2001.

Internet Sites

FactHound offers a safe, fun way to find Internet sites related to this book. All of the sites on FactHound have been researched by our staff.

Here's how:

1. Visit *www.facthound.com*
2. Type in this special code **0736837787** for age-appropriate sites. Or enter a search word related to this book for a more general search.
3. Click on the **Fetch It** button.

FactHound will fetch the best sites for you!

Index